Reading Through History Presents:
History Brief:

The Great Depression:
A Condensed History of America in the 1930s

Jake Henderson

History Brief: The Great Depression
A Condensed History of America in the 1930s
By Jake Henderson
©2016
ISBN-13: 978-1533609175
ISBN-10: 1533609179

Published by:
Reading Through History
Woodward, OK

Table of Contents:

Part One: A Dark Day in Hooverville

Causes of the Great Depression	1
Black Tuesday	4
Hoovervilles & The Bonus Army	8
A Day in the Life of a 1930s Family	12

Part Two: A Tale of Two Presidents

Herbert Hoover	17
Franklin Roosevelt	21
Franklin Roosevelt's 1933 Inaugural Address	25
The First 100 Days	30

Part Three: A "New Deal" in America

The New Deal	33
The WPA	36
The CCC	40
The TVA	44

Part Four: We Interrupt this Broadcast

Radio in the 1930s	48
The Federal Music Project	52
Big Bands & Swing Music	55
War of the Worlds	59

Part Five: No Place Like Home

Movies in the 1930s	63
Bing Crosby	67
Shirley Temple	71
Will Rogers	74

Part Six: Dust Bowl Blues

The Dust Bowl	78
Black Blizzards	81
Dust Pneumonia & Dust Storm Preparations	84
Rabbits, Grasshoppers & Other Problems	87

Part Seven: The Okies

Okies	90
The Grapes of Wrath	93
John Steinbeck	96
Woody Guthrie	100

Part Eight: No One Wears a Crown

Huey P. Long, the "Kingfish"	104
John L. Lewis & the CIO	108
Religion in the 1930s & Father Coughlin	112
"Alfalfa" Bill Murray	116

Part Nine: Women of the 1930s

Eleanor Roosevelt	120
Margaret Mitchell & *Gone with the Wind*	124
Amelia Earhart	128
Babe Didrikson Zaharias	132

Part Ten: The World of Tomorrow

Art in the 1930s	135
Dorothea Lange	138
Federal Theatre Project	141
The 1939 World's Fair	144

This image shows a large number of Model T Fords just off the assembly line, waiting to be sold. The rise of consumerism throughout the 1920s is often seen as one of the causes of the Great Depression, since countless people were making purchases on credit to buy the things they just "had" to have.

Causes of the Great Depression

The 1930s saw a prolonged period of economic difficulties known as the Great Depression. What caused the Great Depression? Could it have been prevented?

In the 1920s, the United States was becoming the world's leading economic nation. The European nations had been devastated by World War I, and America was prospering. The introduction of electricity to American homes had revolutionized day-to-day life. Electric washing machines, vacuum cleaners, irons, radios, and refrigerators were all in high demand.

Increased advertising on radio, and in magazines, only strengthened this desire for new devices. Advertisers were stressing to the American people that they might be the last family on the block to have the latest, greatest product. Americans found themselves *needing* items that, just a few years before, did not even exist.

Unfortunately for consumers, many of these items were too expensive for the average person to buy. A family might have to save for years to purchase a washing machine or an automobile. This led to the development of installment buying, or buying on credit. A consumer would purchase an item by making a small down payment and pay off the rest of the price in monthly installments. This allowed families to own items that they could only dream of otherwise.

Consumers weren't the only ones buying on installment. This same method of purchasing was being used in the stock market. Investors would purchase stocks from a broker, paying as little as 10% of the stock's price. As long as the stock price continued to rise, they could pay off the balance with little difficulty. The stock itself would serve as collateral, meaning if the stock price fell, they would lose the stock and still have to pay off the loan. This method of purchasing stocks was known as buying on margin.

In the 1920s, more and more people were turning to the stock market as a method of making fast income. By 1929, it was estimated that about 4 million Americans were invested in the stock market. Many of these inexperienced investors were also engaging speculation. This meant they were gambling financially with high risk stocks. If the stocks became successful, it meant quick profits. However, speculating on stocks, combined with buying those stocks on margin, could mean financial doom for investors if the stock market took a turn for the worse.

That is exactly what happened in the fall of 1929. In the last week of October, the stock market began to fail.

Nervous investors began to sell their stocks rapidly, which intensified the problem. On October 29, 1929, the stock market collapsed. This day is remembered as Black Tuesday.

Banks were crippled by the stock market crash. In all, 641 banks closed by the end of 1929. More than 5,000 would close in the next several years. Many banks might have survived, but with so many closing, Americans panicked. They hurried to their own bank to withdraw their money, fearing it was about to shut down. This is known as a "run on the bank". With no money to operate with, the bank was forced out of business.

This cycle of disaster only continued. Once consumerism slowed, salespeople were laid off. Many who worked in manufacturing also lost their jobs or had their hours and pay severely cut. As the Depression deepened, millions of these employees were laid off. With no income, the average citizen could no longer afford to repay the debts they had incurred through buying on installment. Since no one was repaying their debts, this crippled even more businesses and financial institutions. The end result was millions more losing their jobs.

<u>Black Tuesday</u>

Most people mark the beginning of the Great Depression with a day known as Black Tuesday. What happened on Black Tuesday? Why is that day so important?

A corporation is a business which individuals buy stock in. The more stock one owns, the larger share of the corporation that person has. These stocks are bought, sold, and traded on the stock exchange (the American Stock Exchange is located on Wall Street in New York City). The success and failure of these corporations is gauged by The Dow Jones Industrial Average. The Dow Jones is an index which shows how large corporations are performing on the stock exchange. If the Dow Jones average goes up, this means that corporations are prosperous, and their shareholders are making money. If the Dow Jones average goes down, this means that many of the corporations are facing economic hardships.

Throughout the 1920s, the Dow Jones Industrial Average had steadily gone up, along with the unprecedented economic growth in the United States. In fact, it had continued to rise for nine years in a row. However, in 1929, the stock market saw major fluctuations. Throughout the year, there were ups and downs as investors bought and sold in sporadic fashion. During the summer months, some economic analysts predicted a major slump, but most did not heed this warning.

Thursday, October 24, 1929 was the first day that saw a dramatic shift. When the stock exchange on Wall Street opened, there was heavy trading, with many choosing to sell their stocks and get out of the market. This caused an 11% drop in the value of the market. A group of leading bankers even held a meeting to see if they might be able to find a solution to the panic that had ensued that day.

Monday, October 28, saw even more activity. The Dow Jones Industrial Average spiraled further downward. This meant that many investors desired to sell their stock, but no one wanted to purchase those stocks for the prices they were being sold at.

The next day, Tuesday, October 29, 1929, was the day that will forever be remembered as Black Tuesday. That day, the Dow Jones Industrial Average fell 30 points, losing 12% of its value. More than 16 million shares were traded, a record that would stand for more than forty years. With so many investors looking to dump their stocks, hysteria ensued, and thousands of

The Great Depression

This was the scene outside the New York Stock Exchange on October 29, 1929, also known as Black Tuesday.

people lost their personal fortunes. The stock market had lost more than $30 billion in value over the course of two days, and the event became known as the Stock Market Crash.

The stock market continued to fall even lower over the next two weeks before finally stabilizing in mid-November. June of 1930 saw another slump in the market, and yet another downward spiral occurred in April of 1931.

Investors had lost faith in the American economy. The decline in stock prices caused bankruptcy and business closures for many corporations. Expansion and innovation became more difficult as no one wanted to invest their financial capital and take risks. As a result, it would take more than a decade for the US economy to recover. This is why Black Tuesday is considered the event that started the Great Depression.

Hoovervilles & The Bonus Army

During the years of the Great Depression, Hoovervilles sprang up across America. What was a Hooverville? Why was it called that?

As the Great Depression continued to get worse, many who had lost their jobs were forced to leave their homes. With no place to live, these individuals, and even entire families, were forced to find shelter wherever they could. In many cases, the only option was for the homeless to construct shacks, or shanties, made out of anything and everything they could find. Boxes, wooden crates, tarpaper, and even old sheets were being utilized as makeshift homes.

Villages of these shacks sprang up in parks and empty plots of land throughout the country. Many cities would not allow the homeless to congregate in this manner, so the shacks would show up on the outskirts of town, or just outside city limits. The term "shantytown" became quite common to describe these types of dwellings. However, because so many in the nation saw President Herbert Hoover as being responsible for the economic woes, a new name emerged. Many people began calling the villages "Hoovervilles".

In 1932, a disgruntled group of homeless World War I veterans decided to create a Hooverville in Washington DC. They placed their little community on the National Mall, in between the Washington and Lincoln monuments. Another Hooverville was set up just across the Potomac River, where it could be seen by those in Washington D.C. Between the two locations, more than 15,000 veterans, their wives, and children had gathered together.

Their purpose was to protest Congress and the president, demanding that they receive money they felt was owed to them. In 1924, the World War Adjustment Act had been passed. This law stated that all veterans would be paid a bonus to make up for the wages they could have been making during the war. Unfortunately, this money was not supposed to be paid until 1944. In the midst of the economic hardships they were facing, these veterans insisted that the money be paid sooner, rather than later. They referred to themselves as the Bonus Expeditionary Force.

The B.E.F. was told by the authorities to disperse and return to their homes. However, many of them didn't have a home to return to. Nearly 2,000 members of this "Bonus Army" refused to leave. President Hoover ordered General Douglas MacArthur to remove them from the city. Using tear gas and rifles, troops

The Great Depression

The "Bonus Expeditionary Force" camping outside the US Capitol Building.

quickly cleared the National Mall before crossing the Potomac to move on the second camp. The nation was in shock. American soldiers had attacked homeless veterans, setting fire to their shacks and huts. The veterans and their families fled Washington DC, but received no better treatment in other places. Virginia, Maryland, and Pennsylvania all instructed them to keep moving along.

Former soldiers, sailors, and Marines, who had once been thought of as heroes, were now viewed as thieves and degenerates. Once again, many saw Herbert Hoover as the source of this dilemma. Voters would express their disgust with the president when they went to the polls in November of 1932.

The "Bonus Army" clashing with police

A Day in the Life of a 1930s Family

Every family was different in the 1930s, but there were some things that many of them had in common. What was day to day life like in the 1930s? What did families do?

A typical family during the Great Depression would have consisted of a father, mother, and several children. The average day would commence with the father of the family leaving for work. That is, of course, if he was lucky enough to still be employed. Shortly after he had left, the children would leave for school. Most children walked to school or rode the school bus.

The mother of the family usually did laundry on Monday mornings. Some families had new, labor-saving washing machines, but washing clothes by hand was still common. The clothes were hung out to dry on a clothes line. Tuesday was ironing day. Some families had electric irons, but many women still used a heavy, black flat-iron that was heated on the stove.

A Day in the Life of a 1930s Family

The most common form of entertainment was the radio. Radio programs would entertain families throughout the day with various kinds of programming. During the day, soap operas would interest mothers while they worked in the home. After school, action and adventure programs for kids were common. In the evening, programs that the entire family might enjoy would take over the airwaves.

If the family didn't want to listen to the radio, they might choose to play a board game, which were becoming popular in the '30s. Sorry! was released by Parker Brothers in 1934 and still remains popular today. By far, the most successful board game was Monopoly. This game gave people the chance to buy and sell property with money they could only dream of having.

A typical 1930s school bus picking up kids before school, or dropping them off at home afterwards.

On Saturday evening, it was common for a family to go shopping, if they had the money to do so. There were a variety of stores downtown, from shoe stores, to clothing, sporting goods, and music shops.

Most families didn't have a lot of money to spend at these stores. The average take home pay was about $17 a week. Some made as little as $7 a week. Doctors made about $60 a week.

The prices of products reflected the economic conditions. A men's shirt cost about $1. A washing machine could be purchased for about $33. A winter coat might cost anywhere from $18 to $28. A milkshake might cost a dime, and a bag of roasted peanuts could be purchased for a penny.

Since many families had so little money, certain things that were once commonplace became luxuries. For example, going to the barber was no longer an option for many families. Haircuts at home became standard practice. Families also stopped going to the dentist for regular check-ups, and doctor visits were saved for very serious conditions. Some women even started giving birth at home in an effort to save money.

Unfortunately, not every family could afford to go shopping or purchase new clothes. Some families were forced to patch shoes with rubber from worn out tires. Even families that had once been affluent began dressing their children in hand-me-downs.

The Great Depression made life extremely difficult for many people. Unemployment rates reached unbelievable numbers, with as much as 25% of the population unable to find work. This meant that an estimated 13-15 million Americans did not have a job.

Those looking for work were desperate. A business would advertise for six positions that needed to be filled and more than 15,000 applicants would apply. Some of those who couldn't find work began riding the rails. Known as hobos, they illegally boarded boxcars on trains, hoping to find work in the next town.

Those who were fortunate enough to keep their job saw their wages slashed by as much as 60%. A worker who had once made $1 an hour would be reduced to 40 cents and be happy to have it. All across the nation, fathers who had once held important positions in companies were now searching dumpsters for their family's next meal.

Food was scarce for many. Cabbage soup became a common meal. Meat and vegetables could no longer be afforded. Some families even resorted to taking turns eating. Some members of the family would eat on Mondays, Wednesday, and Fridays, while others ate on Tuesdays, Thursdays, and Saturdays (with perhaps the entire family eating together on Sunday).

In order to cut heating costs, families resigned to heating only one room of their house. They used many different heating sources, from wood, to coal that they had found, or even corncobs.

In an effort to save money, many families shared homes. Some younger children were sent away to live with relatives in a different part of the country. In other cases, kids as young as 13 were told to leave home and go find work.

Obviously, every family was different, and each had its own set of circumstances. However, each family did everything it could to make it through one of the most difficult times in American history.

An American family in Andersonville, Tennessee, 1933

Herbert Hoover

Herbert Hoover is seen by some as the president responsible for the Great Depression. Who was Herbert Hoover? Did he take any efforts to solve the economic difficulties the nation was facing?

Born in Iowa, in 1874, Herbert Hoover was the son of a blacksmith. He attended Stanford in 1891 and graduated four years later with a degree in Geology. Hoover made his financial fortune as a mining engineer. He made over $4 million mining for silver, lead, and zinc.

The course of his life changed during World War I, though. As the war began, he orchestrated an evacuation of Americans who were trying to get out of Europe and return home. He and 500 volunteers worked to distribute steamship tickets, clothing, and food to more than 120,000 people. Hoover also undertook a relief effort to provide food for the nation of Belgium, which was suffering after the German invasion.

In 1917, President Woodrow Wilson named Hoover

The Great Depression

President Herbert Hoover with his dog "King Tut"

as the head of the U.S. Food Administration. In this position, he organized wartime rationing efforts such as "Meatless Mondays" and "Wheatless Wednesdays". When the war concluded, he shipped massive amounts of food to the starving people of central Europe, even to the defeated nation of Germany. He also sent food to the citizens of Bolshevik-controlled Russia. As the decade came to an end, The New York Times named Herbert Hoover amongst their "Ten Most Important Living Americans".

After Warren Harding was elected president in 1920, he appointed Hoover to the position of Secretary of Commerce. Hoover turned the office into an important position, encouraging "economic modernization" and overseeing everything from air travel to the census. He also started an "own your own home" campaign, which spurred home construction. He is often regarded as the best Secretary of Commerce in U.S. history.

In 1928 he became the 31st President of the United States. This made him one of only two presidents who had never held a previous elected office or high military rank. He had only been president for eight months when the stock market crashed in 1929, which, of course, led to the Great Depression.

He is often criticized for doing little to try and combat the Great Depression. At that time, the United States had a laissez-faire approach to economic matters. This meant that the government did not interfere with economic matters and just left the economy alone. However, Hoover started several public works projects, such as the Hoover Dam, and raised the highest tax bracket from 25% to 63%. He also established the Reconstruction Finance Corporation, which loaned $238 million to banks and railroad companies. Many of the measures Hoover took were similar to efforts Franklin Roosevelt would later make.

Despite these efforts, by 1932, unemployment was over 24%, more than 5,000 banks had failed, and tens of thousands of Americans were homeless. The shantytowns that they developed became known as Hoovervilles, in honor of the president they saw as responsible for their situation.

While Hoover is still viewed by some as "the president who caused the Great Depression", his reputation has improved considerably over the years. He was the last president to hold a full cabinet position prior to being elected, and he also laid much of the groundwork for the New Deal programs of the 1930s.

Franklin D. Roosevelt

The president who oversaw most of the 1930s was Franklin Roosevelt. What did Franklin Roosevelt accomplish as president? Why was he so popular?

Franklin Roosevelt was born in Hyde Park, New York in 1882. His parents were both from wealthy families, and young Franklin lived a privileged life. He was an average student in school, but attended Harvard and graduated with a degree in History.

In 1921, Roosevelt contracted polio. As a result, he became permanently paralyzed from the waist down. In private, he used a wheelchair, but took great lengths to hide his disability from the public. Even while he was president, most Americans did not realize he was unable to walk.

He first made a name for himself in government as the Assistant Secretary of the Navy. He then went on to be elected governor of New York in 1928 (and again in 1930). In 1932, the US was in the midst of the Great

Depression, and Franklin Roosevelt ran for president. He ran on the promise of a "new deal" for the American people and won all but 6 states.

His New Deal programs radically altered the appearance of the nation. Programs such as the WPA, CCC, and TVA put thousands of people to work and helped create the infrastructure of the nation. The WPA built roads, bridges, dams, lakes, and storm drainage sewers. The CCC improved parks, built lakes, planted trees, and created terraces to help fight wind erosion, while the TVA built more than 40 dams in seven Southern states. This prevented flooding in the region and set up electrical power grids to run off of hydroelectricity.

Roosevelt increased the size and scope of government tremendously. His administration created dozens of new government agencies that assumed many different responsibilities. During his presidency, extensive labor laws (such as minimum wage and a 44 hour work week) were also passed, labor unions were strengthened, and the government became a tool to influence and govern the economy.

As the 1930s became the 1940s, Franklin Roosevelt continued serving as president during World War II. His leadership and decision-making ability helped the nation navigate through the war years and become the dominant military power in the world.

Franklin Roosevelt is the only president to serve more than two terms in office. He was elected to the position four times (1932, 1936, 1940, and 1944). This had a dramatic impact on the country and led to the

Franklin D. Roosevelt

passage of the 22nd Amendment to the US Constitution. This amendment states that no president may serve more than two terms.

Roosevelt was not without his critics. Many of his opponents disliked the New Deal, claiming he was leading America down the path of socialism. He was also criticized heavily for his attempt to pack the Supreme Court with justices favorable to his policies. After Congress and the court system began challenging or rejecting many of his New Deal programs, he attempted to increase the number of Supreme Court justices from nine to fifteen. This would have allowed him to appoint all six of the new justices and balance the Court in his favor.

Despite these criticisms, Roosevelt was very popular throughout his presidency and remains so today. There is a monument in Washington DC dedicated in his honor. His image appears on the dime, and there are numerous parks, schools, and other buildings named after him. He is frequently listed amongst the most influential presidents the United States has ever had.

Franklin Roosevelt's 1933 Inaugural Address

March 4, 1933

I am certain that my fellow Americans expect that on my induction into the Presidency I will address them with a candor and a decision which the present situation of our people impel. This is preeminently the time to speak the truth, the whole truth, frankly and boldly. Nor need we shrink from honestly facing conditions in our country today. This great Nation will endure as it has endured, will revive and will prosper. So, first of all, let me assert my firm belief that the only thing we have to fear is fear itself—nameless, unreasoning, unjustified terror which paralyzes needed efforts to convert retreat into advance. In every dark hour of our national life a leadership of frankness and vigor has met with that understanding and support of the people themselves which is essential to victory. I am convinced that you will again give that support to leadership in these critical days.

In such a spirit on my part and on yours we face our common difficulties. They concern, thank God, only material things. Values have shrunken to fantastic levels; taxes have risen; our ability to pay has fallen; government of all kinds is faced by serious curtailment of income; the means of exchange are frozen in the currents of trade; the withered leaves of industrial enterprise lie on every side; farmers find no markets for their produce; the savings of many years in thousands of families are gone.

More important, a host of unemployed citizens face the grim problem of existence, and an equally great number toil with little return. Only a foolish optimist can deny the dark realities of the moment...

... Restoration calls, however, not for changes in ethics alone. This Nation asks for action, and action now. Our greatest primary task is to put people to work. This is no unsolvable problem if we face it wisely and courageously. It can be accomplished in part by direct recruiting by the Government itself, treating the task as we would treat the emergency of a war, but at the same time, through this employment, accomplishing greatly needed projects to stimulate and reorganize the use of our natural resources...

...If I read the temper of our people correctly, we now realize as we have never realized before our interdependence on each other; that we cannot merely take but we must give as well; that if we are to go forward, we must move as a trained and loyal army willing to sacrifice for the good of a common discipline, because

without such discipline no progress is made, no leadership becomes effective. We are, I know, ready and willing to submit our lives and property to such discipline, because it makes possible a leadership which aims at a larger good. This I propose to offer, pledging that the larger purposes will bind upon us all as a sacred obligation with a unity of duty hitherto evoked only in time of armed strife.

With this pledge taken, I assume unhesitatingly the leadership of this great army of our people dedicated to a disciplined attack upon our common problems.

Action in this image and to this end is feasible under the form of government which we have inherited from our ancestors. Our Constitution is so simple and practical that it is possible always to meet extraordinary needs by changes in emphasis and arrangement without loss of essential form. That is why our constitutional system has proved itself the most superbly enduring political mechanism the modern world has produced. It has met every stress of vast expansion of territory, of foreign wars, of bitter internal strife, of world relations.

It is to be hoped that the normal balance of executive and legislative authority may be wholly adequate to meet the unprecedented task before us. But it may be that an unprecedented demand and need for undelayed action may call for temporary departure from that normal balance of public procedure.

I am prepared under my constitutional duty to recommend the measures that a stricken nation in the midst of a stricken world may require. These measures, or such other measures as the Congress may build out of its experience and wisdom, I shall seek, within my constitutional authority, to bring to speedy adoption.

But in the event that the Congress shall fail to take one of these two courses, and in the event that the national emergency is still critical, I shall not evade the clear course of duty that will then confront me. I shall ask the Congress for the one remaining instrument to meet the crisis—broad Executive power to wage a war against the emergency, as great as the power that would be given to me if we were in fact invaded by a foreign foe.

For the trust reposed in me I will return the courage and the devotion that befit the time. I can do no less.
We face the arduous days that lie before us in the warm courage of the national unity; with the clear consciousness of seeking old and precious moral values; with the clean satisfaction that comes from the stern performance of duty by old and young alike. We aim at the assurance of a rounded and permanent national life.

We do not distrust the future of essential democracy. The people of the United States have not failed. In their need they have registered a mandate that they want direct, vigorous action. They have asked for discipline and direction under leadership. They have made me the present instrument of their wishes. In the spirit of the gift I take it.

1933 Inaugural Address

In this dedication of a Nation we humbly ask the blessing of God. May He protect each and every one of us. May He guide me in the days to come.

This image shows Franklin Roosevelt (right) with outgoing president, Herbert Hoover (left), just before Roosevelt's inauguration in 1933.

The First 100 Days

Franklin Roosevelt's administration is famous for accomplishing many things in its "first hundred days". What did he do that was so significant? How did it change the nation?

As Franklin Roosevelt was preparing to enter the White House, he consulted the opinions of several individuals that he had trusted for years. Adolph Berle, Raymond Moley, and Rexford Tugwell were professors at Columbia University and men who had secretly advised the president during his years as governor of New York. These men came to be known as the Brain Trust. Roosevelt would frequently suggest ideas to them and listen to their opinions and advice. While the Brain Trust never officially met during his presidency, the trio undoubtedly had influence over his decision-making process. Roosevelt had other close advisers that he consulted as well, many of whom became a part of administration. Of course, his closest advisor was his wife Eleanor.

When Roosevelt assumed the presidency in March of 1933, his first action was to order all banks to take a holiday for four days. By doing this, he hoped to calm people's anxieties about the banking industry. Fearful citizens had been attempting to pull their money out of banks, believing they would close. This "holiday" gave everyone a chance to calm down, and banks re-opened four days later, with few people rushing to take their money out.

Following that, the new president called a special session of Congress. After Roosevelt had been in office for only four days, the first of the New Deal laws (the Emergency Banking Relief Act) was passed. This was followed by a slew of legislation, most of which occurred from March 20th through June 16th of 1933.

The Economy Act, signed on March 20th, was designed to balance the federal budget by reducing government salaries. The Federal Emergency Relief Act authorized $500 million to provide relief for poor families, in the form of food and clothing. Other major pieces of legislation included the Agricultural Adjustment Act, the Federal Securities Act, and the National Employment System Act.

During the first hundred days, Roosevelt also created the Civilian Conservation Corps, which provided 250,000 jobs for men between the ages of 18 and 25. The Tennessee Valley Authority was also established.

This project would build hydroelectric dams and provide electricity to the Tennessee Valley region.

The "first 100 days" altered the way that many view the office of the president. At the time, many in Washington DC were critical of the new president for doing too much too quickly. However, today an incoming president is often viewed by how much is, or is not, accomplished during the first hundred days of the administration.

Franklin Roosevelt in the early days of this presidency

The New Deal

When Franklin Roosevelt became president, he offered a "New Deal" for the American people. What was the New Deal? How was it put in place?

One of the primary reasons Roosevelt won the presidency in 1932 was because he promised to try and do something to end the economic crisis the country was facing. As he entered the office, Roosevelt hoped to do three things. First, he hoped to provide relief for the poor and the unemployed. Next, he wanted the economy to recover to its normal levels. Finally, he wished to reform the financial systems so that an economic depression would not happen again. Relief, recovery, and reform became known as the three R's.

To accomplish these goals, Roosevelt implemented a series of government programs in between 1933 and 1938. Some of these programs were approved by Congress, while others he enforced through executive order. Collectively, these programs became known as

"The New Deal".

The New Deal is frequently referred to in two different parts. The "First New Deal" (1933-1934) was largely concerned with restructuring the nation's economy and offering relief to the banking industry. The "Second New Deal" (1935-1938) sought to improve the use of the nation's resources, provided relief for farmers, and created various government work programs.

There were many different types of programs that were a part of the New Deal. These programs had a variety of different intended purposes. Programs such as the Works Progress Administration (WPA) and the Civilian Conservation Corps (CCC) were designed to put unemployed people to work. The Social Security Act was created to provide financial relief to the elderly. Meanwhile, the Tennessee Valley Authority brought much needed electricity to rural areas in the South.

The Federal Deposit Insurance Corporation (FDIC) was another important agency created by the New Deal. The FDIC guaranteed the safety of money in banks. Citizens no longer had to fear losing their money if their bank closed (this scenario was quite common in the early stages of the Depression). The FDIC is still in operation today to insure money deposited in banks.

Aside from the FDIC, there are many government agencies that were created by the New Deal which still exist. Amongst them are the Federal Housing Administration (FHA), the Federal Crop Insurance Corporation (FCIC), and the Securities Exchange Commission (SEC).

Not everyone was a fan of the New Deal. Many felt that Roosevelt was leading the United States down the path of socialism. Others saw the New Deal projects as a waste of money and resources. Today, some economists and historians believe that Roosevelt's adherence to New Deal policies actually prolonged the Great Depression.

However, New Deal programs did put millions of people to work, providing economic relief for struggling families. The New Deal initiatives also allowed for the construction of roads, schools, parks, hospitals, and many other facilities that were needed throughout the nation.

The Bonneville Power and Navigation Dam in Oregon was a project built by the Public Works Administration, one of many New Deal programs.

The Works Progress Administration

One of the most ambitious programs enacted by the Franklin Roosevelt Administration during the Great Depression was the Works Progress Administration (WPA). What was the WPA? What kinds of projects were they concerned with?

Created by an executive order from President Roosevelt, the goal of the Works Progress Administration was to provide a paying job for any family whose primary wage-earner was unemployed. Most of the workers the WPA employed were unskilled laborers who were hired for construction projects.

There were many different kinds of WPA projects. Parks, bridges, roads, courthouses, schools, and hospitals were all constructed by WPA workers. Museums, city halls, and swimming pools were constructed as well. To this day, most communities in the United States have a park, bridge, or school that was built by the agency. The program greatly benefited rural areas in the South and western regions of the nation where facilities such as these were desperately needed.

The WPA also assisted women who found themselves unemployed during the Great Depression. The Household Service Demonstration Project trained 30,000 women in skills needed to be a domestic servant (such as a house-keeper or maid). Trainees were taught how to cook, sew, wash and iron clothes, and many other skills that might be needed.

Not all of the WPA programs were for unskilled workers. The Federal Theatre Project, Federal Writers Project, Federal Music Project, and Federal Art Project were all branches of the WPA intended to assist out-of-work authors, artists, actors, and musicians.

Not everyone approved of the WPA. Many felt that such government work programs were a way of introducing communism into the United States. Additionally, some believed that WPA construction efforts were being distributed on a political basis. For example, they claimed that the South received a large number of WPA projects because President Roosevelt was hoping to win votes in that part of the county. Others felt that WPA workers were lazy and developed poor work habits while involved in the program.

1938 proved to be the peak year for the WPA. That year, jobs were provided to more than three million people. Throughout the entirety of the program, the WPA provided short-term labor for eight million Americans.

With the onset of U.S. involvement in World War II

A propaganda poster promoting the Works Progress Administration

in 1941, the need for the program diminished as millions of American men were conscripted into military service. The remainder of the nation's laborers found jobs in American factories, producing tanks and planes for America's war effort. With the need for the program gone, Congress terminated the WPA in 1943.

Over the course of its existence, the WPA constructed more than 40,000 new buildings and improved another 85,000. Amongst these structures were nearly 6,000 new schools and more than 1,000 libraries.

Plaques similar to this can be seen on many buildings throughout the nation which were constructed by WPA workers.

The Civilian Conservation Corps

One of the most popular programs implemented by Franklin Roosevelt as part of the New Deal was the Civilian Conservation Corps (CCC). What was the CCC? Who was it intended for?

The Civilian Conservation Corps was started in March of 1933 as a work relief program. It was intended to provide jobs for young unmarried men, age 18-25, who were out of work due to the Great Depression. By July of 1933, there were 250,000 young men enrolled, working in 1,463 different camps.

When one became a member of the CCC, he signed a commitment to participate in the program for a minimum of six months. At the conclusion of this time period, he could choose to enlist for another six months. The maximum limit was a total of four terms (or two years) that one could stay in the program.

Each enlistee was required to take a physical examination prior to joining. Physical fitness was important

The Civilian Conservation Corps

Propaganda poster promoting the Civilian Conservation Corps.

because of the demanding labor that would be involved.

Each CCC worker was given meals, housing, a uniform, and thirty dollars a month. Twenty-five of the thirty dollars was sent home to their parents. The workers lived in camps and were housed in barracks (fifty workers to a tent). Aside from the barracks, the CCC camps also featured an education building, a medical facility, a mess hall, a recreation area, restrooms and showers, a tool room and blacksmith shop, and garages.

The primary function of the CCC was to conserve natural resources and clean up the national parks and forests. Their very first projects related to soil erosion control in Alabama. Soil erosion projects became especially important in the Great Plains states, which were being ravaged by the Dust Bowl. One of the most important CCC projects was re-forestation (planting trees). The trees were needed to serve as wind blocks, which helped control the soil erosion problem.

Before long, CCC camps were all over the country, tackling many different kinds of tasks. CCC projects included everything from building fire lookout towers, roads, and airport landing fields, to controlling insects and diseases, fish stocking, and eliminating predatory animals. They also constructed terraces, built dams, and established campgrounds.

By 1940, the program started being reduced significantly. The Great Depression was approaching its end, and there was less need to employ young workers. In 1941, when the United States entered World War II, this need became even less, because most men of this age were either enlisting or being drafted to help in the war effort. The program was officially ended on June 30, 1942.

At the time of its conclusion, the CCC had employed over 2.5 million young men. They had built over 97,000 miles of road, constructed more than 800 parks, and planted more than 3 billion trees.

CCC workers take a break from their work to pose for a photograph

The Tennessee Valley Authority

During the 1930s, there were few regions of the country that were worse off than the region known as the Tennessee Valley. Where is the Tennessee Valley? How did the New Deal help this area?

The area known as the Tennessee Valley includes portions of Tennessee, Alabama, Mississippi, Georgia, and Kentucky. For years, this region was far behind the rest of the nation in many areas of life. Electricity, running water, sewers, and proper sanitation were all elements of our modern life that were sorely lacking in the Tennessee Valley during the 1930s. One of the major goals of many New Deal programs was to help modernize the South and improve living conditions in those states.

The most notable of these New Deal programs became known as the Tennessee Valley Authority (TVA). The TVA's goal was to build hydroelectric dams throughout the area, which would bring electricity into thousands of homes. Eventually, the TVA would construct and maintain more than 30 hydroelectric dams that provided inexpensive power to millions of Southerners. In 1933, it was estimated that only 2% of homes in the Tennessee Valley had electricity. By 1945, this number had been improved to 75%.

Bringing electricity to the region was extremely important. Not only did home appliances and electric lighting make life easier, but there were other benefits as well. Factories and other businesses were now able to locate in the region and employ thousands of workers.

The Ocoee Dam No. 1 was one of many hydroelectric dams maintained by the Tennessee Valley Authority. These dams helped bring electricity to many Southern communities.

There were also health benefits to the increased availability of electricity. Better lighting meant improved eyesight and a reduced risk of accidents. Electric refrigerators allowed Southerners to keep food longer without it spoiling. This meant they could purchase food from the grocery store, rather than depending on homegrown produce and dairy products.

Electricity also meant that Southerners could purchase what the rest of the nation had been enjoying for the past decade or more, a radio. The radio proved very meaningful in the isolated Tennessee Valley region. It helped Southerners feel more connected to the rest of the nation. They could now listen to the same news and radio programs that people from New York to Los Angeles were listening to.

Aside from providing electricity, the TVA was also concerned with soil conservation. The organization promoted the use of fertilizers and crop rotation to improve soil conditions. The TVA also had programs to improve fish and wildlife habitats, control wild fires, and replant forests.

The TVA was not always popular. The construction of the hydroelectric dams caused more than 15,000 families to lose their homes. Those areas were flooded to make lakes and reservoirs. Also, many Southerners were suspicious of government officials. Therefore, the TVA had to recruit local citizens to speak to their neighbors about soil conservation techniques.

Other New Deal programs were created to help fight diseases. Hookworm, pellagra, malaria, typhoid, and diphtheria had long plagued the South. These diseases were spread through poor sewage and sanitation systems (which allowed germs and bacteria to spread rapidly). New sewer systems in major cities helped reduce the number of deaths caused by diphtheria and typhoid. New water treatment facilities also improved the condition of drinking water.

Swamp drainage in South Carolina resulted in a 16% drop in malaria cases, and mosquito eradication efforts helped reduce malaria-related deaths by 66%. There were similar successes in reducing the number of cases of dysentery, hookworm, and pellagra.

This sign displays the logo used by the TVA

The Great Depression

Radio in the 1930s

The most popular form of entertainment in the 1930s was radio. What were some of the most listened to radio programs? Who were the biggest radio celebrities of the day?

Radio burst onto the scenes in 1920 and quickly became a national craze. No other new product caught on as quickly as radio. Everyone wanted to have one in their home. Two years after radios went on the market, radio sales were bringing in more than $60 million a year.

Radios came in all shapes and sizes too. The least expensive models could be purchased for about $8. A nice radio might cost about $50. The most expensive radios on the market were the size of a chest-of-drawers and cost more than $500! By the dawn of the 1930s, about half of the homes in the country had a radio. There were also more than 500 radio stations operating in the United States.

Radio networks quickly developed programming to entertain their listeners. During the workday, when most listeners were housewives, romance and drama programs were featured. *The Romance of Helen Trent*, *Stella Dallas*, and *Life can be Beautiful* were all popular programs. These shows were usually sponsored by products that housewives needed, such as laundry soap. Thus, these programs became known as "soap operas".

The after school hours were usually filled with action and adventure programs for kids. *Flash Gordon*, *Hop Harrigan*, *Sky King*, and *Superman* were amongst the most popular. These programs usually ran 15 minutes and kept children engaged while their mother prepared the evening meal.

In the evening, everyone would gather around the radio and listen to programs the entire family might enjoy. *The Lone Ranger* and *Amos & Andy* were both popular evening programs. Shows such as *The Shadow* would hook listeners with popular catch phrases like "Who knows what evil lurks in the hearts of men? The Shadow knows!"

One of the most popular programs of the 1930s was hosted by Jack Benny. However, it was not known as the *Jack Benny Show*. As many programs of that era were, the show was named after the product that sponsored it. In this case, the show was known as *The Jell-O Program*. With the rapid growth of radio's popularity, companies had been quick to realize how effective it could be for promoting products. Medicines, food, soft drinks, coffee, and even cars were all advertised on the

The Great Depression

This image shows a family listening to the radio. By 1930, 50% of all homes had a radio, and there were more than 500 radio stations across America.

radio.

Stations also realized how effective radio could be as a source of news. Radio listeners of the era grew accustomed to the phrase "we interrupt this broadcast..." which was usually followed by a breaking news bulletin. As technologies improved, many stations even featured a live "man on the scene" who would report about events taking place.

Probably the nation's best known voice on the radio in the 1930s was that of President Franklin Roosevelt. Throughout the decade, he offered periodic radio addresses known as "Fireside Chats". These addresses were intended to assure the nation that, although times were tough, things would get better.

The Federal Music Project

One of the more interesting New Deal programs was known as the Federal Music Project. What was the Federal Music Project? How long did it exist?

Many musicians were hurt badly by the Great Depression. During a time of such economic hardship, there were fewer and fewer people hiring live musicians or paying to attend concerts. These types of performances were considered luxuries, which the average family could no longer afford. Additionally, new technological advancements in recording techniques, primarily records and record players, lessened the need for live musicians.

In 1935, the Federal Music Project (FMP) was created with the goal of employing as many out of work musicians as possible. They would work as instrumentalists, singers, and performers, entertaining people across the nation. Aside from employing the musicians, the project had two other goals. First, they hoped to provide a much needed distraction for common people who were suffering through the economic crisis. Also, they hoped to bring a higher level of culture and sophistication to their audiences. Because of the economic hardships, admission to these concerts was offered at very inexpensive prices, or, oftentimes for free.

The FMP had other projects as well. Aside from entertaining the masses, the FMP also intended to educate them. Trained musicians working for the FMP offered music instruction to adults who could not afford private lessons. It also created community orchestras and choirs, as well as starting music programs for children. The FMP became so successful that most schools in the nation had their own music program.

A group of children singing in an FMP choir

The final mission of the FMP involved researching, collecting, and preserving America's musical heritage. FMP workers scoured the country to record or write down every song they could. Every type of music was catalogued from hillbilly, to jazz, folk, Creole, gospel, and African American.

Unfortunately, like many of the other New Deal programs, the Federal Music Project's budget was reduced in 1939. That same year, the project was renamed the WPA Music Program. A year later, it was terminated all together.

The Federal Music Project lasted only four years, but it was quite successful in that time. FMP musicians performed thousands of concerts for millions of people. There were also more than 30 orchestras created across the nation, as well as countless local singing groups. Perhaps most importantly, the music of the nation's common people was collected and preserved for future generations.

Big Bands & Swing Music

In the 1930s, many young Americans began listening to swing music. What was swing? Who were the major performers?

Big band music was all the rage in the 1930s. "Big bands" were jazz or swing bands, usually composed of about 12 to 25 musicians. The instrumentation usually included saxophones, trumpets, trombones, clarinets, drums, and a stand-up bass.

One of the earliest stars of the swing era was Duke Ellington. Ellington was a composer, pianist, and bandleader who became famous in the late 1920s. In 1926, he and his group became the house band at the famous Cotton Club in New York City. The Cotton Club was an exclusive place with wealthy clientele. However, each week there was a regular radio broadcast from the Cotton Club, which gave Ellington national exposure. Ellington remained one of the most popular figures in music throughout the 1930s, producing classics such as

"I Got it Bad", "Mood Indigo", and of course, "It Don't Mean a Thing (If It Ain't Got That Swing)."

Another dominant figure of 1930s swing music was Benny Goodman. In fact, Benny Goodman earned the reputation as the "King of Swing". Goodman was a clarinetist and the leader of his own swing band. Goodman became incredibly popular in the latter half of the 1930s.

The seminal event for 1930s swing music occurred on January 16, 1938. It was a concert known as *Benny Goodman at Carnegie Hall*. The King of Swing took the stage along with Duke Ellington, Count Basie (another famous bandleader), Gene Krupa (a famous drummer), and many other musicians. They performed for hours in front of a sold-out Carnegie Hall. This concert is regarded by many as the moment when jazz and swing music gained full acceptance by mainstream audiences.

Swing music also produced several dances. The jitterbug was an incredibly popular dance craze throughout the 1930s. The Lindy Hop was also very popular in the late 1920s and early '30s. Swing even produced an entire form of dance, swing dance, which remains popular today.

Those who followed swing music closely even developed their own slang language. Terms such as "hipster", "hepcat", and "jive" all became commonplace. "In the groove" and "jam session" were popular as well. Many of these terms have been added to the modern lexicon and are still used today.

Swing music is seen as significant not just because of

Benny Goodman was one of the most popular big band leaders and was known as the "King of Swing"

the quality music that was produced. It is also viewed as important for helping to break down racial barriers. White audiences were enjoying the music of African American performers, and musicians of various races were taking the stage to perform together.

Today, Duke Ellington, Benny Goodman, and many other swing performers are remembered amongst the greats of American popular music. Their music is enjoyed to this day, and many current musicians claim them as musical influences.

Duke Ellington became one of the most prominent "big band" leaders

War of the Worlds

The "War of the Worlds" broadcast was one of the most memorable events to occur in the 1930s. What happened during this broadcast? Who perpetrated this stunt?

On October 30, 1938, the Mercury Theatre Radio Group aired a dramatic radio presentation of the classic HG Wells novel *The War of the Worlds*. The novel conveys the story of an alien invasion of Earth. The group conducting the broadcast presented the story in a modern setting and changed the stage to New York and New Jersey (the original novel took place in England).

The story was presented in real time, as if the events were actually taking place. Regular music programming was periodically interrupted with "special bulletins" which informed the listeners of the latest news regarding the alien invasion. Many people heard these reports and believed the invasion was really happening.

At the beginning of the broadcast, there *was* an announcement stating that the program was a radio drama. Unfortunately, many people missed this announcement. Thousands of listeners called the police. Some went outside and convinced themselves that they could see flashes of light in the distance as the "battle" ensued. Others were certain they could smell poisonous gases being fired by one side or the other.

There were incidents of hysteria all across the country. Many people rushed into the streets with shotguns and rifles, ready to battle the unknown alien enemy. Others fled to the hills, trying to escape the cities.

The situation was made increasingly worse because the broadcasters were using real place names. For example, the initial alien landing was supposed to have taken place at Grover's Mill. Crowds of people arrived at this location with guns and other weapons. As a result, the police and fire department were forced to go there and manage the crowds. Bystanders who saw the mass of armed citizens, police, and firemen had no choice but to believe that the rumors of alien invasion were true.

It has been estimated that approximately 6 million people listened to the broadcast and, of those, up to 1 million may have believed the events were actually happening. Orson Welles, the 23-year-old director of the program, was largely unaware of the public's reaction. He and his fellow performers were simply trying to present an entertaining radio program.

Today, there is much debate over how many people

Orson Welles addresses reporters in the aftermath of the "War of the Worlds" broadcast.

were genuinely panicked. Many of the stories about hysteria were exaggerated by newspaper articles which appeared in the days that followed. In fact, despite the thousands who might have been frightened, there were indeed millions who listened to the program and were thoroughly entertained.

However, the *War of the Worlds* broadcast did have a major impact. The broadcast helped Americans appreciate how effective radio could be for news broadcasts. Many people also learned the valuable lesson of not believing everything they heard on the radio.

War of the Worlds told the story of an alien invasion

Movies in the 1930s

Movies were becoming a major part of day-to-day life in America during the 1930s. Who were the most popular film stars of the era? What did the movies mean to the people in that decade?

In 1927, a movie titled *The Jazz Singer* debuted. This was the first movie to feature sound (all movies prior to that had been silent films). Ever since that time, the film industry has been a booming business in the United States. Even in the 1930s, during the Great Depression, 80 million movie tickets were sold every week.

There were many big-name stars throughout the decade including Errol Flynn, James Cagney, and Edward G. Robinson. Cagney and Robinson were best known for their roles in gangster movies like *The Hatchet Man* (Robinson) or *G-Men* (Cagney). America became fascinated with young actors and actresses like

Mickey Rooney, Judy Garland, and of course, "America's little darling" Shirley Temple.

The biggest movie star of the decade was Clark Gable. From 1930 to 1939, he made thirty-nine movies. He portrayed many different types of characters, from a cowboy, to a gangster, reporter, chauffer, gambler, lawyer, doctor, minister, and miner. However, he will always be best remembered for his role as Rhett Butler in the 1939 film *Gone with the Wind*.

Gone with the Wind remains one of the most popular and most critically acclaimed movies of all time. It grossed nearly $200 million in theaters. This made it the most financially successful movie ever made, a record it held for 26 years. When adjusted for inflation, it remains the most successful film of all time.

1939 is often regarded as the greatest year in cinematic history. Aside from *Gone with the Wind*, several other notable films were released that year. *Wuthering Heights* (starring Laurence Olivier), *Mr. Smith Goes to Washington* (featuring Jimmy Stewart), *Stage Coach* (with John Wayne), and *The Wizard of Oz* are still regarded as classics today.

Movie theaters of the 1930s were grand, elegant structures. Many theaters had chandeliers or other luxurious features in the lobby. The seats in each theater were nice and plush, and the screen was behind an ornate curtain that opened when the movie started.

Each movie began with a newsreel, previews of coming attractions, and a cartoon. These animated shorts introduced moviegoers to characters such as Bugs

Movies in the 1930s

The Wizard of Oz was one of many classic films released in the year 1939. In this photo, the cast is seen in costume portraying their legendary characters. From left to right: The Cowardly Lion (Bert Lahr), Dorothy (Judy Garland) The Scarecrow (Ray Bolger), and the Tin Woodsman (Jack Haley).

Bunny, Mickey Mouse, Daffy Duck, Donald Duck, and many others. Other live-action shorts might have featured the Three Stooges or the Little Rascals.

In the afternoons, many theaters showed a matinee. These were cheaply-made films intended for children. Most were science fiction or cowboy films. Many of these movies were serials, meaning each film would end in a "cliff-hanger", and young viewers would have to return the following week to see the conclusion. Matinees were usually priced lower, with tickets costing as little as 10 cents. In the evening, ticket prices averaged about 25 cents, and theaters showed higher quality films intended for the entire family.

Movies meant a great deal to the people living through the Great Depression. It was not merely a form of entertainment or a way to pass the time. Going to the movies provided much needed relief from the struggles of daily life. Many people were poor, and times were tough, but for 25 cents, they could enter a beautiful theater and forget their worries for a couple of hours.

Bing Crosby

Bing Crosby was a figure of popular culture for nearly three decades. Who was Bing Crosby? What did he do to become so famous?

In 1903, in Tacoma, Washington, Harry and Kate Crosby gave birth to a son, Harry Crosby Jr. When young Harry was six, he earned the nickname "Bingo". Over the course of time, the "o" was dropped from this nickname, and he simply became known as Bing Crosby.

Bing became involved in music while in high school. He played drums for a short-lived band made up of other high school students. After high school, he moved on to quick success, singing with Paul Whiteman's Orchestra for $150 a week. He then became the featured singer of the Rhythm Boys. It was with this group that Bing sang his first #1 hit, a jazz version of "Ol' Man River."

Crosby made his solo debut in September of 1931,

The Great Depression

Bing Crosby

and he quickly became known for his distinctive vocal talents. His deep baritone voice entranced millions of listeners. By the end of 1931, ten of the top 50 songs on the radio featured Bing Crosby.

In 1932, Bing starred in his first feature movie. The film was titled *The Big Broadcast* and was the first of many films starring Crosby. Bing would go on to become as well-known for his acting abilities as he was for his singing talent.

Crosby also had one of the most popular radio shows. Starting in 1936, he began hosting the Kraft Music Hall on the NBC Radio Network. He held this position for the next ten years, entertaining listeners across America, as well as abroad.

During the years of World War II, Bing's broadcasts were transmitted to troops fighting in Europe and the Pacific. These broadcasts were also heard by countless German troops who became fans as well, calling him "Der Bingle". Crosby also flew to Europe and made a number of live appearances for soldiers stationed there. Between his broadcasts and live performances, he boosted the morale of many soldiers and helped them feel a little closer to home.

Bing Crosby's legacy as a performer is virtually unmatched. As a singer, he recorded more than 1,700 songs. Forty-one of those reached #1 on the popular music charts. His most famous recording is the song "White Christmas", which remains the best-selling song of all time.

Crosby is also one of the most successful actors of all-time. He appeared in a total of 79 films. More than 1 billion tickets were sold to see movies starring Bing Crosby. By this measure, it ranks him as the third most successful actor of all-time, behind Clark Gable and John Wayne. He won the Academy Award for Best Actor for his role in *Going My Way*. He was also nominated for the award on two other occasions. Many of his films are regarded as classics today, and they can still be seen on television.

Bing Crosby died on October 14, 1977, but he will continue to live on in the hearts and minds of people around the world for years to come. A song was once written in tribute to Bing which stated "Bing has a way of singing with his very heart and soul, which captivates the world. His millions of listeners never fail to rejoice at his golden voice."

Crosby sings "White Christmas" with Marjorie Reynolds in Holiday Inn *(1942)*

Shirley Temple

During the 1930s, a young actress named Shirley Temple delighted movie-goers throughout the nation. Why was Shirley Temple so popular? How is she remembered today?

Shirley Temple was born in 1928 and started acting almost as soon as she could walk. Her first acting roles came in 1932 when she was only three years old! By 1934, she became a leading star. The movie *Stand Up and Cheer!* brought her to national attention. That same year, the film *Bright Eyes* featured the song "On the Good Ship Lollipop", which became her signature song.

Throughout the rest of the decade, Shirley Temple became one of the biggest stars in Hollywood. She starred in twenty different films from 1934 to 1939. *The Little Colonel*, *Curly Top*, *The Littlest Rebel*, *Dimples*, *Heidi*, and *The Little Princess* were just a few of the movies that propelled her to international fame.

The Great Depression

Shirley Temple

Most of her film roles were very similar. She was always the little girl with the bright smile who could win over the hearts of the stingiest misers and soften the most calloused of individuals. She could reunite couples or solve any other problem that came along. The movies always featured many song and dance numbers in which Shirley could showcase her talents. These heart-warming stories provided much needed inspiration for many viewers who were enduring the woes of the Great Depression.

Throughout the 1930s, many products were marketed featuring Shirley's likeness. From Shirley Temple dolls to mugs and cereal bowls, she was everywhere. Other items that bore her name included a line of Shirley Temple dresses, soap, sheet music, mirrors, and numerous other products.

Temple remained an active actress throughout the 1940s and 50s, appearing in a number of films and television programs. However, she would never be as successful as she was during the decade of the 1930s. She retired from acting and became an ambassador for the United States. She was ambassador to Ghana from 1974 to 1976 and then to Czechoslovakia from 1989 to 1992.

Shirley Temple died in February of 2014 at the age of 85. To this day, she remains one of the most beloved performers in the history of the motion picture industry. Her films are still cherished by millions of adoring fans, and she will continue to live on as a beloved piece of American history.

Will Rogers

One of the most enduring figures of the 1930s was Will Rogers. Who was Will Rogers? What did he become famous for?

Will Rogers was born in 1879 in Indian Territory, near present-day Oologah, Oklahoma. His parents were both part Cherokee. He was the youngest of eight children, but only three of his siblings survived into adulthood.

In 1901, Rogers heard that there was money to be made in Argentina. So, he and a friend headed out in search of their fortunes. When they arrived in Argentina, they discovered that the money they dreamed of was a myth. So, his friend went back to Oklahoma, but Will stayed. From there, he got a job on a boat that was headed for South Africa.

In South Africa, he went to work on a ranch and was eventually hired by Texas Jack's Wild West Show. He appeared in the shows as "The Cherokee Kid" and became famous for performing rope tricks. He toured South Africa with the Wild West Show until he was hired by a circus that took him to Australia and New Zealand.

In 1904, he returned to the United States and started performing vaudeville in New York City. Vaudeville was a form of variety show which usually featured singers, dancers, jugglers, comedians, and other performers. Rogers performed his tricks and told jokes to the audience as he twirled his rope. The sophisticated New York audiences loved Will's country accent. He also had a natural sense of humor that crowds appreciated. Rogers would often open each show by saying, "All I know is what I read in the papers". He would then joke about current events and poke fun at political figures of the era.

By 1916, he was the star of the biggest show in New York, the Ziegfeld Follies. He also began acting in silent films, which only increased his celebrity status. In his films, he sometimes portrayed cowboys, or perhaps comedic characters similar to himself. He continued acting in films up through 1935, eventually starring in over fifty movies.

Rogers also started writing weekly newspaper columns in 1926. Over the course of his writing career, Will wrote more than 4,000 columns which were syndicated in newspapers all over the world. Additionally, he hosted a weekly radio program in which he told jokes and discussed many different issues that were relevant

The Great Depression

Will Rogers

to people of that time period.

One of Will's favorite topics was the advancement of commercial aviation. He believed that airplanes were the future of travel, and he spoke about the subject frequently. He flew to every destination he could in an effort to prove how safe traveling by plane could be.

It was this love of aviation which eventually caused his death. In 1935, he embarked on a journey with his good friend Wiley Post (a pilot who had become famous for flying around the world). The two were attempting to fly over the Bering Strait from Alaska to Russia. Somewhere over Alaska, their motor stalled and the plane crashed, killing both men. Will Rogers' death was mourned by the entire nation. Kings and presidents from foreign nations even expressed their regrets at his passing.

Today, Will Rogers is remembered as an American legend. Buildings, streets, and even an airport have been named in his honor. There is also a statue of him standing in the U.S. Capital Building.

The Dust Bowl

The Dust Bowl was a severe period of drought and dust storms throughout the 1930s. Why did the Dust Bowl happen? How severe was the damage?

The earliest explorers to the Great Plains region of North America determined that the area was unsuitable for agriculture. The territory even became known as "The Great American Desert" because the lack of trees and water made the region relatively unattractive for settlement. However, in the decades following the Civil War, farmers began to settle the region and cultivate the fields under the long-held, but mistaken, belief that "rain will follow the plow."

In the first three decades of the 1900s, there were significant and continuous advances in farming technology, including better tractors, mechanized plowing, combines, and more. From 1900 to 1920, the amount of farmland in the plains region doubled, and from 1925 to 1930, the amount of cultivated land tripled!

However, farmers of the era used practices which deprived the soil of its nutrients and increased the possibility of erosion. The heavy plowing had eliminated the natural grasses of the prairie that held the soil in place and maintained moisture.

Then, in 1930, a severe drought struck the Great Plains region, which lasted nearly the entire decade. The regions affected most by this drought were the panhandles of Texas and Oklahoma, western Kansas, and large portions of Colorado and New Mexico. The more than one million acres that was affected became collectively known as "The Dust Bowl".

As the drought grew worse, the topsoil turned to dust and blew away. The blowing dust generated enormous dust storms that reached as far east as Washington D.C.! The dust storms became known as "black blizzards".

During the decade of the 1930s, the Dust Bowl region received anywhere from 15-25% less precipitation than normal. For a region that only sees about twenty inches of rain a year, this means that some areas were receiving as little as fifteen inches of rain in one year (in some years, even less than that!).

As the decade wore on, and the severity of the Dust Bowl increased, efforts were made to correct the conditions. The Civilian Conservation Corps planted more than 200 million trees from Texas to Canada in an attempt to block the wind and hold the soil in place.

Farmers were also instructed in soil conservation techniques such as crop rotation, contour plowing, and terracing. In some cases, the government even paid farmers a dollar an acre to practice one of these conservation techniques. By the end of the 1930s, they had succeeded in reducing the amount of blowing dust by 65%.

By the time the rainfall returned to normal levels, nearly 75% of the topsoil had been blown away in some areas. It would be years before the region recovered completely.

A South Dakota farm in 1936 that has been buried in dust and dirt

Black Blizzards

During the 1930s, dust storms ravaged the Great Plains region. The worst of these became known as Black Sunday. When did Black Sunday happen? Just how bad was it?

In the early part of the 20th Century, over-farming, poor soil conservation techniques, and excessive livestock grazing had created a dangerous situation. The topsoil of the Great Plains region had been stripped of its nutrients, as well as the natural vegetation that had once held the soil in place.

Then, 1930 saw the first year of what would eventually be an eleven year drought, in which precipitation (in the form of rainfall, snowfall, and other forms of moisture) was just a fraction of the normal levels.

These factors combined to dehydrate the soil and turn it into a fine, powdery dust. The wind picked up large amounts of this dust and generated massive dust storms which swept across the plains. The storms could reach more than 10,000 feet in height and produce winds from 50 to 80 miles per hour. The storms came to be known as "black blizzards".

The dust storms began in the early 1930s and continued to progress in severity and in number as the decade wore on. In 1932, there were at least fourteen major dust storms, by 1935 there were more than forty, and 1937 saw more than seventy. Historical records of the era were not kept accurately, and some speculate that there may have been more than one hundred dust storms in one year.

The worst of these dust storms occurred on April 14, 1935. The storm blew away an estimated 300 million tons of topsoil in just a few days. The sky became so filled with dirt, that the sun could not be seen. Some witnesses described the event as "a wall of dirt that the eyes could not penetrate". This storm became known as "Black Sunday".

A dust storm moving in on a farming community

The dust storms affected more than just the Great Plains region. Eastern cities such as Chicago, New York City, Boston, and Washington DC also experienced these massive storms. The skies became so dark that street lights were needed during the day time, and there are even reports that the snow was red in Boston (because the snow was mixing with the soil from a dust storm). Even sailors in the Atlantic Ocean report finding as much as a quarter-inch of dust on the decks of their ships from these massive storms.

Citizens across the nation lived in fear of when the next dust storm would come. As the events became much more commonplace, many learned to recognize the origin of the dust storm by the color of its dirt. Brown dust storms were from Kansas or Nebraska, gray from Texas, and red dust storms were from Oklahoma.

By the late 1930s, the dust storms began to reduce in number. Increased use of soil conservation methods, as well as much needed rainfall, helped to bring the dust storms to an end. However, the damage that had been done was irreparable. Scientists estimate that roughly 30 billion tons of the most nutrient-rich topsoil in the world had simply blown away.

Dust Pneumonia & Dust Storm Preparations

One of the worst health conditions from the Dust Bowl era was dust pneumonia. What was dust pneumonia? What methods did Dust Bowl residents use to try and combat the encroaching dust?

During the 1930s, when the Great Plains region was being plagued by a drought and ravaged by dust storms, a new physical ailment emerged. It was known as dust pneumonia, and it was caused by breathing in dust from the air. Dirt would fill the lungs and cause coughing, tightness of the chest, labored breathing, and shortness of breath.

Children and the elderly were affected the most, with deaths being common. Many were hospitalized because of this condition, but it is difficult to tell exact numbers because medical records from the era were either not kept, or not well preserved.

Those who lived in the Dust Bowl tried many methods to combat the dust and keep themselves healthy.

Dust Pneumonia & Dust Storm Preparations

A man and his children seek shelter during a dust storm

Parents would have their children sleep with sheets over their beds, like a tent, to reduce the amount of dust they inhaled during their sleep. Dust masks and wet cloths over the mouth were other methods that some used to try and prevent dust inhalation. Additionally, goggles were sometimes worn to keep blowing dust out of the eyes.

Housewives made many efforts to keep the dirt and dust out of the home. Sometimes these activities were as simple as constantly sweeping the floors. Other methods were more significant, such as tacking bed sheets in front of doors and windows, wetting them down in an effort to keep out as much dust as possible. They also used strips of cloth, soaked in a paste made of flour and water, to insulate the outer edges of windows, trying to seal them shut.

While humans could take these measures, animals were not so lucky. Cattle and other livestock had little shelter and nowhere to run from the dust storms. Many families were forced to watch helplessly as their animals died from dust inhalation. No livestock meant no meat, eggs, milk, or other dairy products, which only added more hardship to their lives.

The dust was everywhere. Residents of the Dust Bowl region lived in it, breathed it, slept in it, and even ate it (many Dust Bowl survivors testify that they could feel the gritty dirt in their food). There was no escaping it. The measures mentioned above helped reduce the dust some, but it was a constant presence in their lives.

Rabbits, Grasshoppers & Other Problems

The dirt and dust storms of the Dust Bowl era were just the beginning of farmers' problems in the 1930s. What were some of the other problems they faced?

As a severe drought ravaged the Great Plains, and the huge dust storms further altered the ecology of the region, new waves of pests began sweeping across the prairie.

The worst of these new varmints were jackrabbits. Jackrabbits breed at an amazing rate, producing as many as eight young a month. Normally, jackrabbit populations are kept at normal levels because of their natural predators such as coyotes. However, during the Dust Bowl, those predators had either died, or moved on to other regions in search of water.

With no natural predators, the jackrabbit population surged to unbelievable levels, and they became a major pest across the plains as they ate grass and crops. In an effort to reduce the jackrabbit population, residents across the Dust Bowl region held rabbit drives, rounding up the animals and disposing of them. In one rabbit drive, which took place in Kansas, they captured more than 35,000 rabbits in one afternoon.

Grasshoppers became another nightmare during the Dust Bowl. Just like the jackrabbits, the grasshopper's natural predators (birds and rodents) had moved on in search of water. Grasshoppers travelled in swarms across the land, with as many as 23,000 insects per acre. They devoured virtually everything in their path. Many efforts were utilized to try and curtail the plague of grasshoppers. The National Guard burned infested fields and even crushed the insects with tractors. The Civilian Conservation Corps spread large amounts of insecticide which was made from arsenic, molasses, and bran.

Swarms of grasshoppers were a major pest

Inside houses, other types of insects were a danger as well. Poisonous centipedes and deadly spiders infiltrated homes in search of shade or water. There are some reports of women filling entire buckets full of these types of pests.

Static electricity created a different type of danger. Friction caused by blowing dust particles rubbing together, and against metal objects, created large amounts of static electricity. This electricity was powerful enough to kill crops and even knock a person unconscious. Many Dust Bowl survivors remember seeing blue arcs of static electricity at night, coming from windmills and barbed wire fences. These were just a few of the additional dangers that many people endured during the Dust Bowl.

Centipedes were another common pest

Okies

As the Dust Bowl made life increasingly difficult for those living in the central plains, many people decided to abandon their homes in search of new opportunities. Who were these people? Where did they go?

Many left the Dust Bowl region in favor of trying to find a job in the city. Others decided to leave the area altogether. Most of those who left had a common destination, California. Writers of the era observed that the highways between Oklahoma and California resembled a parade, with a continuous string of cars heading west. Others compared it to the gold rush of 1849, with millions of migrants moving in search of a fresh start.

In 1934 alone, Oklahoma lost more than 400,000 people. That same year, Kansas lost over 200,000. The plains states as a whole experienced a loss of 2.5 million people. Oklahoma suffered the most in terms of population loss. Other states lost 3% or 4% of their population, but some estimates claim that Oklahoma lost as much as 18% of its total population.

Not all of the Dust Bowl refugees were from Oklahoma, but because so many of them were, the Californians had a nickname for all of them. They called them Okies. Journalist Ben Reddick first used the term "Okie" in his articles after noticing the "OK" abbreviation on many of the migrant license plates.

Most of these Okies were heading to California because they thought they could find jobs picking fruit. After all, California supplied nearly half of the fresh fruit for the entire country. However, there were multiple downsides to this occupation.

First, there were far more workers than were needed. With such a surplus of laborers, employers could pay extremely low wages (there was no minimum wage at that time). Additionally, many jobs only lasted two or three days, at which point the worker needed to move on to the next location in order to find more work. This forced the Okies into a migratory lifestyle, constantly moving on to the next orchard, grove, or vineyard.

Given the migrant lifestyle and low pay, the Okies lived a very hard, unpleasant life. They were looked down upon by Californians and many towns refused to permit them entrance. They were forced to live outside of communities in makeshift villages of shacks and other poorly built shelters. These places became known as Little Oklahomas. Because these communities were filthy, with little proper sanitation and no running water, diseases such as typhus and diphtheria became widespread.

To help expose the plight of the Okies, a writer named John Steinbeck wrote a book in 1939 titled *The Grapes of Wrath*. This novel told the story of Tom Joad and his family as they traveled from Oklahoma to California and their hardships once they arrived.

Eventually, the U.S. government attempted to help the Okies living in California. Camps were organized to provide better toilet and bathing facilities as well as community cooking areas and laundry rooms. By 1941, there were 13 of these camps across California with about 45,000 people living in them.

The nickname "Okie" was originally used by Californians as an insult. In *The Grapes of Wrath*, the main character Tom Joad observed, "Okie means you're scum." However, in modern times, many people from Oklahoma have embraced the nickname and use it with pride, just as a Hoosier from Indiana or a Yankee from New England uses those nicknames.

A migrant family on its way to California

The Grapes of Wrath

In 1939, John Steinbeck wrote a novel which would become one of the most controversial books of all time. It would also become one of the most celebrated works of American literature. What was this novel? Why was it so controversial?

The Grapes of Wrath focuses on the Joad family, poor share-croppers from Oklahoma who have to leave their home because of the Dust Bowl and the other economic hardships associated with the Great Depression. In an effort to change their luck, they set out for California, along with thousands of other Okies.

The book was first published on March 14, 1939. By May, it was at the top of the best sellers list, and by the end of 1939, almost 500,000 copies had been sold. Its price of $2.75 was fairly reasonable at the time, which allowed many people to purchase copies. Even those who had never read a book before were buying it. Book stores were sold out, and there were waiting lists at libraries that were months long.

The book paints an incredibly vivid picture of the hardships endured by the Dust Bowl's migrant workers. It also illustrates how the migrants were treated after arriving in California. When people read it, they were shocked by the poverty and hopelessness presented in the story.

However, not everyone liked what they were reading. There were claims that the book exaggerated the hardships of the Okies. Many declared that it was impossible for such horrible circumstances to exist in the United States of America. Also, citizens of California were displeased with the way Steinbeck portrayed the Californian attitude towards the migrants. The Associated Farmers of California denounced the book as a pack of lies.

Some criticized the novel for other reasons. It emphasized cooperative solutions to economic problems instead of individualistic solutions. Because of these themes, many people felt it was pro-socialist or pro-communist.

Because of the book's controversial nature, it was banned from many libraries across the country. One group in California called for "widespread denouncement against the book before school opens and our boys and girls find such filthy material on the shelves of our public library."

National radio programs debated the merits of the book, and it was even publicly burned in Buffalo, New

York; East St. Louis, Illinois; and in several communities in California. Oklahoma Representative Lyle Boren went as far as denouncing the book in Congress as a vulgar lie. However, much of this uproar died down when Eleanor Roosevelt praised the book and defended Steinbeck.

In 1939, *The Grapes of Wrath* won the Pulitzer Prize for a Novel, and the popularity of the book has endured to this day. John Steinbeck's novel has been translated into many different languages including French, German, and Japanese.

The Grapes of Wrath remains banned in many school libraries across the nation. However, it is probably the most discussed and debated American novel of the 20th Century and will always be considered one of the classics of American literature.

A migrant family on their way to California, similar to the Joad family in The Grapes of Wrath

John Steinbeck

John Steinbeck was one of America's greatest authors. What books did John Steinbeck write? Why were they so popular?

Raised in California, John Steinbeck formed an appreciation for the region. In particular, he grew to love California's Salinas Valley, which greatly influenced his writing. As a teenager, Steinbeck made the decision to become a writer and often locked himself in his room to do his writing. In 1919, Steinbeck enrolled at Stanford University, but eventually dropped out in 1925, having never graduated.

Steinbeck briefly moved to New York City where he found work as a newspaper reporter, but the pull of California quickly drew him back home. While working as a caretaker in Lake Tahoe, he wrote his first novel, *Cup of Gold*, in 1929. Over the next decade Steinbeck wrote *The Pastures of Heaven* and *To a God Unknown*, both of which were poorly received by critics.

John Steinbeck

Steinbeck eventually achieved success with *Tortilla Flat* in 1935, a humorous novel about life in the Monterrey region. The book was very popular, selling more than 26,000 copies in its first year (during the heart of the Depression). Two years later, Steinbeck published *Of Mice and Men*. This novel tells the story of two migrant ranch workers. Much of the book is based on Steinbeck's own experiences traveling the country as a hobo. *Of Mice and Men* remains enormously popular and is read in classrooms across the nation.

The Grapes of Wrath was published in 1939. The novel relays the tale of a Depression-era Oklahoma family and their struggle to create a new life in California. In many minds, it perfectly captured the mood and discontent of the nation during this difficult time. At one point, *The Grapes of Wrath* was selling 10,000 copies a week! It also earned Steinbeck a Pulitzer Prize in 1940.

Following the success of *The Grapes of Wrath*, Steinbeck served as a war correspondent during World War II. He continued to write for the rest of his life, producing classics such as *Cannery Row* and *East of Eden*. He was even awarded the Nobel Prize for Literature in 1962.

John Steinbeck died of heart disease on December 20, 1968, but left behind a monumental legacy that included 27 books. Over a ten year period, he produced several of America's greatest masterpieces of fiction. He will always be remembered for writing about social and economic issues while giving voice to working-class

America. He is one from an elite list of authors who had a gift for creating characters that were relatable to a broad, general audience.

Woody Guthrie

Unquestionably, the most enduring musical figure to emerge from the Dust Bowl era was a man named Woody Guthrie. Why was Woody so popular? What kind of songs did he sing?

Woody Guthrie was born in Okemah, Oklahoma in 1912. His father was the first County Clerk in Okfuskee County. By the standards of the day, his family was an average, middle-class family.

At the age of six, Woody's sister died tragically in a kitchen accident. Not long after, his mother was stricken with Huntington's disease. Doctors of the time were unfamiliar with the disease, and as a result, she was placed in a mental institution.

When Woody was 19, he moved to Pampa, Texas and started performing with a band known as the Corn Cob Trio. However, in 1935, he packed up his belongings and headed west with the rest of the "Okies".

Woody Guthrie

Along the way, he rode in box cars and jalopies, going from Oklahoma, to Kansas, Colorado, and California. During his journeys, he lived amongst the migrant workers, singing to them and about them. He sang to people who were always too hot, too cold, too hungry, or too poor. He sang old hymns and folk songs, which comforted the migrants and reminded them of home and of simpler times.

He also wrote his own music. Many of the songs he wrote were hard-hitting social commentaries about what he saw going on around him: the hardships people were facing, the unemployment, the hunger, and the diseases which ravaged them.

As time progressed, the themes in his songs continued to become increasingly politicized. Much of his music advocated the sharing of wealth. He eventually became famous as a voice for the working class and a champion of worker rights. Many criticized his songs for these themes, and some even accused him of being a communist.

Woody genuinely believed in the ideals he sang about. He didn't believe in the personal ownership of his own music. He always said, "These songs didn't cost me anything to write, so you can have 'em if you want 'em." He also gave much of the money he made to those who needed it.

Throughout his years living in California amongst the migrant workers, he held many different jobs. He painted signs, picked fruit, and washed dishes. He hosted a weekly radio show out of Los Angeles where he was billed as "Oklahoma Woody". He even wrote a weekly newspaper column called "Woody Sez…"

In 1940, Woody left California and traveled to New York City. It was there that he wrote his most famous song "This Land is Your Land" as a protest song. It was also in New York where he finally recorded many of the songs he had been singing for years. RCA made a collection of Woody Guthrie music known as *Dust Bowl Ballads*.

Unfortunately for Woody, he began exhibiting some of the early symptoms of Huntington's disease, the same illness which had inflicted his mother. By the early 1950s, his condition was so bad that he was no longer able to perform, and he spent the final years of his life in and out of the hospital. He died in 1967 at the age of 55.

Woody Guthrie changed the world of American music forever. He was one of the first extremely influential singer-songwriters in American history. He inspired countless other songwriters who followed him, and he continues to do so today.

The Kingfish

Throughout the Great Depression, there were many people looking for answers. They were prepared to follow anyone who might have an easy cure for the nation's woes. One of these men was Huey P. Long. Who was this man? What were his solutions?

During the 1930s, many politicians, labor leaders, and preachers were making a name for themselves. They used everyone's fear, anxiety, and anger as a tool to climb through the ranks of power. Many of these leaders became known as "demagogues". The most prominent of the demagogues was Huey P. Long, nicknamed "the Kingfish".

Huey Long was born in 1893. He grew up in a very poor region of Louisiana, yet his own family was quite well off. He studied law at Tulane University and jumped right into politics at an early age. He ran for governor in 1924 and lost, then ran again in 1928 and won. In 1930, he ran for the U.S. Senate and won that too! By 1935, he was easily the most powerful man in the state of Louisiana.

Economic conditions were terrible in Louisiana in the 1930s. Long accomplished much of his success by appealing to poor farmers and factory laborers with a "poor against the wealthy" mentality. He also delivered on many of the promises he made during his campaign. These promises included paving roads and building public schools. He informed his followers that 65% of the nation's wealth was controlled by 2% of the population. He preached a message that "every man is a king, but no one wears a crown," and used the slogan "Share the Wealth".

Long argued that there should be limits placed on how much wealth a person could acquire. Anything beyond that level would be redistributed to others. He believed that every deserving family should be given $5,000. He promised that under his system, every family would be guaranteed an annual income of $2,000 to $3,000, a 30 hour work week, one month of vacation a year, old age pensions, and free college education for deserving students.

Suddenly, "Share the Wealth" clubs began springing up all over the country. There were more than 27,000 clubs with over 4.6 million members. He received thousands of letters of support from across the nation. As the Kingfish's message continued to spread, he began to set his sights on the big prize— being elected President of the United States. Long was not only popular in his home state, but had large amounts of support throughout the country.

However, on September 8, 1935, Long had returned

Huey P. Long, the "Kingfish"

to Louisiana. As he was walking towards the governor's office, a man in a white suit stepped out from behind a pillar and fired a single shot into Senator Long. Long's bodyguards opened fire and gunned down the assassin, leaving 61 bullets in the gunman's body. Long was rushed to a hospital where he died 30 hours later.

Tens of thousands of Louisianans turned out for the Kingfish's funeral. His death was mourned by people across the nation. He was buried on the grounds of the state capitol building, which now has a statue featuring his likeness. He has also been honored with a statue in the United States Capitol Building.

This photo of Long was taken in 1935 about two weeks prior to his death.

John L. Lewis

One of the most influential labor leaders of the 1930s was John L. Lewis. Who was John L. Lewis? How did he become so influential?

John L. Lewis was born in Iowa in 1880. His father was a coal miner, and Lewis himself went to work in the coal mines when he was only 16. He became active in the coal miner's union and eventually worked closely with Samuel Gompers (the founder of the American Federation of Labor).

In the 1930s, there were few industries as important as the coal industry. However, coalminers were not allowed to join the AFL because it was created for "skilled laborers" and coalminers were "unskilled laborers". As a result, Lewis formed the Congress of Industrial Organizations (CIO). This was a conglomerate labor union made up of other labor unions which all represented unskilled workers. This included not only coalminers, but rubber workers (who made tires), steel workers,

John L. Lewis

auto workers, and many others.

The CIO supported many groups of striking workers in the late 1930s. One of the biggest strikes of the decade was a strike by the United Auto Workers. The General Motors factories in Flint, Michigan and Cleveland, Ohio were virtually shut down by the striking workers. Before the strike, the GM factories had been producing 15,000 cars a week. During the strike, this number dropped to just over 150. GM was eventually forced to negotiate with its striking workers for better wages and safer working conditions.

This was just one of many strikes which occurred in the latter half of the 1930s, all of which were backed by John L. Lewis and the CIO. Other strikes took place in steel mills, tire factories, shoe factories, aircraft factories, and even bakeries. Many of these strikes were not traditional strikes, in which workers walked out, or protested on picket lines. Instead, they used a new method of striking known as the sit-in, or sit-down strike.

The workers would occupy their usual workspace, but simply refuse to work. This had the advantage of making it difficult for police or National Guard to remove them, and it made it virtually impossible for the workers to be replaced. It also increased camaraderie between the workers as they were living together inside the factory for days, or even weeks (for example, the GM factory strike lasted 44 days!). In an effort to pass the time during the sit-in, workers would play cards or listen to the radio. One strike even featured a band which performed for the striking workers (the band itself was made up of workers). Meals would be brought in by wives or friends who were supporting their cause.

Through these efforts, the workers experienced a new sense of power. They were able to effect change in their condition and provide a better working environment and higher wages for their fellow workers.

Many of these strikes were made possible, or heavily supported, by the efforts of John L. Lewis and the Congress of Industrial Organizations. Lewis would continue to be a major figure in American labor for the next two decades. He is remembered today as one of the most important figures of the 20th Century labor movement.

1930s Religion & Father Coughlin

The era of the Great Depression saw an increase in the practice of religion. Why did this increase occur? Who was the major leader of the movement?

As economic hardships continued to worsen throughout the 1930s, many people began to hold tightly to their religion. For them, conditions had become so miserable that their only hope was that something much better awaited them after death. Religion became an emotional stabilizer and helped many people through the difficult times.

Between 1929 and 1937 there was a sharp rise in all of the Protestant denominations of Christianity. Methodists, Baptists, Lutherans, and many other churches all experienced a staggering increase in membership. Catholic church attendance was on the rise as well. Several new religious organizations, such as the Jehovah's Witnesses, also emerged during the 1930s.

Millions of people found comfort and safety within

Father Charles Coughlin was one of the most listened to voices on the radio during the 1930s

the church community. Historically, providing aid to the poor had always been a mission fulfilled by churches. Soup kitchens, food and clothing donations, and other relief efforts were all organized by various religious groups throughout the nation.

One of the leaders of this new religious fervor was Father Charles Coughlin. Father Coughlin served as the priest for a Catholic church in Michigan known as the Shrine of the Little Flower. He also hosted a radio program known as *The Radio League of the Little Flower*. As the 1930s progressed, Father Coughlin became one of the most listened to voices on the radio.

In 1936, his radio-sermons were broadcasting on 35 different radio stations. It was estimated that he had approximately 30 million listeners tuned in each week to hear his weekly sermons. This gave him much influence over the political situation of the era.

Initially, Father Coughlin supported Franklin Roosevelt and the New Deal efforts. However, as time progressed, Coughlin became more outspoken against the president. Coughlin also utilized his program to attack communists, labor unions, banks, the Supreme Court, and many other political opponents.

Father Coughlin announced the creation of a new political party, the Union Party, in 1936. He also announced that he would run for president as a Union Party candidate. His bid for the nomination was unsuccessful, but this did not diminish the influence Coughlin had over his followers.

In the late 1930s, a group known as the Christian

Front emerged. They claimed Father Coughlin as their inspiration, although he had no direct connection to the group. Thousands became members of the organization and started secretly conducting drills with rifles. Groups of "Fronters" roamed the streets of major cities, attacking Jews and other groups they disliked.

The FBI arrested seventeen Fronters in 1940. In the Fronters' possession, the FBI found bombs, dynamite, weapons, and stockpiles of ammunition. The FBI claimed that the group had plans to assassinate prominent Americans and seize post offices and armories. Despite the evidence against them, the members of the Christian Front were acquitted of the charges and set free.

Alfalfa Bill Murray

One of the most charismatic and controversial governors of the 1930s was Governor William H. Murray from Oklahoma. What did Murray do to become so well-known? Why did he become controversial?

William H. Murray was born in Toadsuck, Texas on November 21, 1869. The family moved to Montague, Texas after his mother died and his father remarried. At the age of twelve, young Bill decided to leave home. He was eventually adopted by another family who had him attending school in the winter and working on farms during the summer.

As he got older, he worked as a salesman, a teacher, a newspaper reporter, and a lawyer. But, he was first and foremost a farmer. He always liked to tell people that he "believed in the family farm, the values of Thomas Jefferson, and the greatness of the Democratic Party."

In 1898, Murray moved to Tishomingo, which was

the capital of the Chickasaw Nation in Indian Territory. He became involved in politics while living in Indian Territory and served as one of the representatives at the Sequoyah Convention. This was a meeting which attempted to create a state out of Indian Territory (the eastern half of present-day Oklahoma).

Murray was also president of the constitutional convention when Oklahoma finally became a state in 1907. He was the state's first Speaker of the House, a member of Congress, and he ran for governor twice and lost, all before 1924. Bill Murray seemed to be a constant figure in Oklahoma politics. In many of his speeches, he frequently referred to a plot of land which he grew alfalfa on. One newspaper referred to him as "Alfalfa Bill" in a column. The nickname stayed with him throughout the remainder of his life.

Then, in 1924, Murray and his wife led a group of American colonists, most of them Oklahomans, to Bolivia. Once they were in Bolivia, they attempted to establish an agrarian colony. The attempt failed miserably, and only five years later, in 1929, they returned to Oklahoma.

Alfalfa Bill had lost all of his money in the effort. So, he borrowed $40 from a bank in Tishomingo and started a campaign for governor. Murray traveled across the state in a worn-out car, stopping at street corners to give speeches. He ate his lunch out of a paper bag while talking about politics with anyone who would listen. He was frequently unshaven and his clothes were dirty. He presented himself as a down to earth

The Great Depression

William H. "Alfala Bill" Murray

common man. He won the 1930 election by more than 100,000 votes, becoming Oklahoma's ninth governor. This was the largest victory of any Oklahoma governor up to that time.

During his career as governor, Murray called out the National Guard on 47 occasions and declared martial law 30 times. The most famous of these was the two month incident known as the "Toll Bridge War". In the summer of 1931, Oklahoma National Guardsmen faced off against Texas Rangers over a "free bridge" that had been built across the Red River to replace an older toll bridge. When the governor of Texas, Ross Sterling, sent Rangers to barricade the Texas side of the new bridge (as part of a court injunction), Governor Murray sent National Guardsmen to remove the barricades and keep roads to the bridge open. The Texas injunction against the new bridge was eventually dissolved.

As governor, Murray became one of the early national leaders in the effort to help those hurt by the Great Depression. He used his own salary to feed the poor and collected money from state employees and businessmen to finance relief programs to aid those suffering during the economic crisis.

Alfalfa Bill's popularity even carried him onto the national scene. In 1932, he attempted to become the Democrat nominee for president. He participated in several primary elections, but eventually lost the nomination to Franklin D. Roosevelt.

Eleanor Roosevelt

Eleanor Roosevelt was one of the most influential First Ladies in American history. What did she do that changed the role of the First Lady? How did she impact American life?

Eleanor Roosevelt was raised in New York City. Her family was extremely wealthy, but her early life was not without its difficulties. Both her mother and father died before she was 10. When Eleanor was 18, she met her future husband, Franklin, while traveling on a train. Eventually, the two were engaged, and they married on March 17, 1905.

Eleanor's role in politics began as early as 1921 at the onset of Franklin's polio. She would fill in for him at public appearances when he was incapable of travelling. She also became a strong advocate for such goals as minimum wage, a 48 hour work week, and the abolition of child labor.

She became very influential in the New York State

Eleanor Roosevelt

Democrat Party. The ties she made amongst other important Democrat women helped her husband secure the nomination for governor and go on to win the election. Of course, being the governor of New York eventually led him to the presidency.

As First Lady, Eleanor's goal was to redefine the position. She became the most active First Lady in history and established the modern standard for what is expected from the role. She began holding her own press conferences (holding 348 during her twelve years in the White House). She also had a daily newspaper column, which she wrote six days a week from 1936 to 1962. She spoke all over the country at various speaking engagements, earning $1,000 a speech, and even co-chaired the Office of Civilian Defense.

All of these activities helped her to champion the role of women in American society. She became so active and involved in her husband's administration that it began to alter the public's opinion about women. This was significant during an era when few women had employment outside of the home. Also, at her weekly press conferences, she banned male reporters. This forced newspapers to hire female reporters in order to keep up with Eleanor's activities. This act placed women in positions where they could voice their opinions about issues.

Aside from being a champion of women's rights, Roosevelt was also a major advocate of African American rights, being very outspoken with her support of the Civil Rights Movement. In fact, she became so popular amongst African Americans that it helped create a significant shift in the voting demographics of the nation. African Americans had long been a solid voting base for Republicans. However, this began to shift in the late 1930s, partially due to Eleanor Roosevelt's stance on civil rights issues.

Eleanor Roosevelt meeting with Shirley Temple

Margaret Mitchell & Gone with the Wind

One of the most widely-read novels of the 1930s was Gone with the Wind. *Who wrote this novel? Why was it so popular?*

Margaret Mitchell lived her entire life in Atlanta, Georgia. She was born into a wealthy family in 1900. Her father was a lawyer, and her mother was a suffragist who fought for women's rights.

Margaret was a tomboy who preferred riding ponies over playing with dolls. When she was little, she would go riding nearly every day with a Confederate veteran. At the age of six, Margaret's mother took her on a tour of many of the plantations that had been burned, or otherwise destroyed, during the Civil War. As a child, she also spent much time around uncles who were Civil War veterans and aunts who had lived through the conflict. These elderly relatives told her many stories about the war and how difficult those times had been.

When Margaret was 22, she took a job as a journalist

Margaret Mitchell

at the *Atlanta Journal*. Her family did not approve of this career, as they felt being a writer was beneath her status in society. She worked for the *Atlanta Journal* for four years, writing more than two hundred articles.

Then, in 1926, she was involved in an automobile accident which severely injured her ankle. While recovering, her husband encouraged her to write a novel. She continued to work on the manuscript for the next ten years. Finally, in 1936, the novel was published. It was titled *Gone with the Wind*.

Gone with the Wind tells the story of Scralett O'Hara, the daughter of a wealthy plantation owner, who finds herself in poverty in the aftermath of the Civil War. It's a coming-of-age story that details the struggles of Scarlett's life as she grows from adolescence into adulthood.

The novel was immediately successful, becoming the best-selling book of both 1936 and 1937. People across America, especially women, were reading *Gone with the Wind*. It resonated with many who had experienced prosperity during the 1920s, but found themselves suffering in the midst of the Great Depression. In 1937, Mitchell received the Pulitzer Prize for fiction. Two years later, the film version was released starring Clark Gable and Vivien Leigh. The film was a smashing success, setting box office records that would stand for decades.

The novel would eventually be translated into more than seventy languages. Foreign audiences appreciated the story for its themes of love, war, class conflict, racial strife, and generational conflict, which are universal to the human condition.

To this day, the novel is still loved and cherished by millions of readers throughout the world. It is thought of as one of the greatest American novels ever written, and a book that helped influence and shape the nation.

The Crescent Apartments, in Atlanta, Georgia, is where Margaret Mitchell wrote Gone With the Wind. *It is now known as the Margaret Mitchell House & Museum.*

Amelia Earhart

One of the most famous female pilots who ever lived was Amelia Earhart. What did Amelia do to become so well-known?

When Amelia Earhart was about 20 years old, she attended the Canadian National Exposition in Toronto. While there, she watched an aerial demonstration by a World War I pilot and became fascinated by airplanes. Two years later, in 1920, her father paid $10 for her to take a 10 minute flight that changed her life. During this flight, she decided that she must learn how to fly airplanes for herself. At the cost of $1,000, she signed up for flying lessons.

She quickly proved to be a talented pilot and even set a world record. In 1922, she became the first woman to fly at an altitude of 14,000 feet. The next year, she received her pilot's license, becoming only the sixteenth woman to do so.

Over the next several years, she did a considerable

Amelia Earhart

amount of flying. In 1928, she became the first woman to cross the Atlantic Ocean in an airplane. However, she was not the pilot on this trip. She served as the navigator for pilot Wilmer Stultz. That same year, she also became the first woman to fly solo across North America. These daring feats easily made her the most famous female pilot of her day. One newspaper referred to her as "Lady Lindy" (comparing her to Charles Lindbergh), while another called her "The Queen of the Air". She quickly grew to be one of the chief spokespersons for the aviation industry.

On May 20, 1932, a 34-year-old Amelia Earhart took off from Harbour Grace, Newfoundland. She traveled for nearly 15 hours, facing fierce north winds, mechanical difficulties, and hazardous, icy flying conditions. She touched down just north of Derry, in Northern Ireland. Her landing was only witnessed by two farmers. She had just become the first woman to fly across the Atlantic Ocean on a solo flight.

In 1937, Earhart decided she would attempt to fly around the world, something no woman had ever done. She made her first attempt on March 17, 1937. Her plane took off in Oakland, California but only made it as far as Honolulu, Hawaii before experiencing mechanical difficulties. The flight was called off and rescheduled.

The second attempt came on June 1, 1937, this time departing from Miami, Florida. She and her navigator, Fred Noonan, had traveled more than 22,000 miles when something went horribly wrong. Somewhere in the middle of the Pacific Ocean, they realized they were hopelessly lost. On the morning of July 2, 1937, Amelia Earhart sent out her last radio message at 8:43 AM, indicating that they were running low on fuel. A massive search lasted for seventeen days, but no wreckage was ever found. Earhart and Noonan were never heard from again.

Amelia Earhart was unsuccessful in flying around the world, but her name is still remembered today. She was the first woman to fly solo across the Atlantic Ocean, and she inspired a generation of women to achieve great heights in many different fields.

Babe Didrikson Zaharias

One of the most notable athletes of the 1930s was Babe Didrikson Zaharias. Who was Babe? What sports did she become famous for?

Babe Didrikson's real name was Mildred, but almost everyone remembers her as "Babe" (a lifelong nickname). Her parents were Norwegian immigrants, and she had six brothers and sisters. When she was four years old, her family moved to Beaumont, Texas where she would grow up. She wasn't a great student and even dropped out before finishing high school.

Fortunately for Babe, she was an extremely talented athlete. When she was 21, she gained worldwide attention at the Amateur Athletic Union (AAU) Championships in July of 1932. In less than three hours, she competed in eight different events, winning five and tying for first in a sixth. She set three world records that day, including the javelin, 80m hurdles, baseball throw (which she threw 272 feet), and the high jump. Later that month, she competed in the 1932 Summer Olympics in Los Angeles. She won two gold medals (the hurdles and javelin throw) and a silver for the high jump.

After the Olympics, she began a career in golf. Throughout the late 1930s and 1940s, Babe Didrikson was the dominant name in women's golf. She was unquestionably America's first female golf superstar. She accomplished many feats throughout her career, including being the first American to win the British Ladies Amateur. At one point she won as many as thirteen tournaments in a row!

In 1938, she married a professional wrestler named George Zaharias, becoming Babe Didrikson Zaharias. The two met while at a charity golf event and wed less than a year later. The couple remained married for the rest of Babe's life.

Aside from being a gifted track athlete and golfer, Babe Zaharias experienced great success in other sports as well. She played baseball and softball, was a skilled diver, a bowler, and she also excelled at roller-skating. She also found time to be an excellent seamstress, sewing all of her own golf outfits. She could even play the harmonica and sing (she recorded songs for Mercury Records!).

In 1953, Babe was diagnosed with colon cancer. She battled the illness for two years before finally losing the struggle in 1955. She died at the age of 45, but managed to continue playing golf right up to the end of her life.

The Great Depression

At the time of her death, she was still the #1 ranked female golfer in the world.

In her lifetime, she won the Associated Press "Female Athlete of the Year" six times. In 1999, the Associated Press named her the "Greatest Female Athlete of the 20th Century". However, her impact goes far beyond her exploits in sports. She was one of many females throughout the 1930s and '40s that changed the public's expectation of women. In a society where many believed that women should be "getting themselves prettied up and waiting for the phone to ring," (in the words of one sportswriter from that era), she was proving that women not only had a place in society, but a place in sports as well.

Babe Didrikson Zaharias

Art of the 1930s

There were many different works of art produced throughout the 1930s. What were some of these works? Who were the important artists of the era?

One of the most iconic paintings of the 1930s is titled *American Gothic*, and it features a farmer and his wife. It was painted by Grant Wood in 1930. Wood and several others were associated with a painting style known as regionalism in which they portrayed scenes from rural life. Other painters, like Edward Hopper, became famous for painting scenes from urban life.

Unfortunately, not all artists could afford to support themselves through their work. The Great Depression had taken a great toll on the art community. With little extra income to spend, paintings and sculptures were considered luxuries. In 1935, the Federal Arts Project was created as part of the New Deal. Its primary goal was to employ out-of-work artists. In exchange, the artists provided art for government buildings. To this day, courthouses, schools, hospitals, and post offices display wall murals created as a part of this program.

Others were employed to design and create poster art for New Deal programs. The Federal Arts Project also employed sculptors and photographers. The photographic division took thousands of photos of contemporary life as well as pictures of WPA workers in action.

Aside from this, the Federal Arts Project had another mission as well. The organization had an Art Teaching Division which held classes to teach art. These artists taught nearly 8 million students and adults in schools and community centers across the nation.

Young African Americans learn to paint in a class provided by the Federal Art Project

The Federal Arts Project existed until 1943. During that time, artists working for the organization produced more than 2,500 murals, 18,000 sculptures, and countless other pieces of artwork. At the height of its activity, it employed more than 5,000 artists, some of whom would go on to successful careers, including Jackson Pollack.

Architecture took on an artistic twist as well in the 1930s. Starting in 1925, a new, dramatic, sleek style of design was introduced in Paris. It became known as Art Deco. Before long, the Art Deco influence had spread across the Atlantic to America, and it could be seen everywhere. Buildings were not the only things being constructed with an Art Deco look, everything from chairs, to telephones, radios, and even ashtrays were being viewed as pieces of art. Automobiles and trains also began to exhibit a more streamlined design that was influenced by Art Deco.

The top of the Chrysler Building serves a good example of the art-deco style of architecture

Dorothea Lange

Some of the most stunning photographs from the 1930s were taken by Dorothea Lange. Who was Dorothea Lange? Why was she taking all those pictures?

Dorothea Lange was born in New Jersey in 1895. When she was seven years old, she contracted polio, which permanently weakened her right leg. As a result, she walked with a limp for the remainder of her life.

She attended Columbia University where she took classes in photography. She eventually opened a portrait studio in San Francisco, but when the Great Depression struck, Lange began photographing the homeless and unemployed she saw arriving in California.

Her photographs of Dust Bowl refugees attracted the attention of government agencies, and she was eventually employed by the Farm Security Administration (also known as the Resettlement Administration). She, along with her husband, Paul Schuster Taylor, continued to document the destitute individuals they encountered over the latter half of the 1930s. Taylor was an economics professor who collected data while Lange photographed the people.

Many of Lange's photographs helped bring the plight of the poor to national attention. The photos appeared in newspapers and magazines across the country. Her most famous photo is entitled "Migrant Mother", which shows a distraught woman and her children.

In 1942, just after the Japanese attack on Pearl Harbor, thousands of Japanese Americans were being forced to relocate into internment camps. Once again, Lange was there with her camera. She preserved images of Japanese Americans who had committed no crime but were being detained by their own country. The US Army disapproved of her photographs and impounded them for thirty years.

Lange went on to accept a position teaching photography at the California School of Fine Arts. Through the remainder of her life, she struggled with a number of health problems, including bleeding ulcers. She also suffered from renewed symptoms related to her bout with polio. She died in 1965 at the age of 70, following a battle with esophageal cancer.

Dorothea Lange has been remembered in various ways. A school near the spot where she photographed the "Migrant Mother" has been named in her honor. She has also been inducted into the California Hall of Fame. Of course, her most lasting legacy will always be the images she captured during the 1930s and '40s, which will continue to serve as haunting reminders of those troubling times.

Dorothea Lange

Federal Theatre Project

One of the most controversial New Deal programs was the Federal Theatre Project. What was the Federal Theatre Project? Why was it controversial?

The Federal Theatre Project (FTP) was organized in August of 1935. Its goal was to employ as many out-of-work actors, directors, and artists as possible. Aside from employing the actors and other performers, the Federal Theatre Project also had the secondary mission of entertaining the nation. Actors, singers, and dancers performed shows all across America, providing a much needed escape from the economic realities of the Great Depression.

In its four years, it employed 12,700 workers in 31 different states. This program not only employed actors, but producers, directors, and script writers as well. Carpenters were employed to construct sets, seamstresses were hired to design costumes, and unskilled

A poster advertising the Federal Theatre Project's play titled One Third of a Nation.

workers were brought in to be ticket-takers or work behind the scenes in many other capacities.

Several actors, writers, and directors who worked with the FTP would go on to greater fame later in their careers. Arthur Miller, John Houseman, and Orson Welles are just a few of the names who participated in FTP projects. Houseman and Welles, along with Marc Blitzstein, collaborated on the controversial FTP production titled *The Cradle Will Rock*.

The FTP produced more than 1,200 plays and put on a thousand performances a week. An estimated 30 million people saw FTP-produced plays. This gave the organization an extraordinary amount of influence over American opinion. This is why the organization became controversial as time progressed.

Some felt that the plays and musicals produced by the FTP were far too politically opinionated. There were those in Congress who did not feel that a government agency should be producing what they believed was propaganda. For example, one production was extremely critical of the Supreme Court. Another production promoted worker rights and encouraged laborers to go on strike. One play, *Revolt of the Beavers*, was criticized for being pro-communist. *Revolt of the Beavers* was particularly troubling to many because it was targeted specifically at children.

It was the controversial nature of these productions which eventually led to the end of the FTP. Congress disapproved of the program and cancelled its funding on June 30, 1939.

The World of Tomorrow

In 1939, the New York World's Fair gave spectators a glimpse at the "world of tomorrow". What was the World's Fair? What types of displays were there?

Throughout the 1930s, there were many expositions and "world's fairs" across the nation. One of the first occurred in Philadelphia in 1926. It was called the Sesquicentennial International Exposition and celebrated the 150th anniversary of the nation's independence. Chicago held a similar event in 1933 known as the Century of Progress Exposition. California hosted two world's fairs. The first was in 1935, in San Diego, and it was known as the California Pacific Exposition. The second came in 1937 and was called the Golden Gate Exposition, with the featured attraction being the newly constructed Golden Gate Bridge.

The biggest and best of the world's fairs was the New York World's Fair which opened on April 30, 1939. The fair covered nearly two square miles and had several

The World of Tomorrow

Two of the featured attractions at the 1939 World's Fair were the Perisphere and Trylon. Inside the Perisphere was a model of the "city of the future". The sphere was entered by an escalator and once inside, one would move about along a "moving walkway". The Trylon was 610 feet tall. The two structures were connected by an escalator.

zones, including Transportation, Communications, Food, Government, Community Interests, and Amusement.

The theme of the fair was "The World of Tomorrow", and each of these different zones displayed what the future might look like in each respective field. For example, in the Transportation Zone, General Motors showed off a model city designed for cars with superhighways from coast to coast and no red lights. Ford displayed some of their newest vehicle designs.

In other exhibits, fair attendees received a glimpse of television for the first time. Color photography was also on display for all to see. General Electric introduced the world to the fluorescent light bulb, and one auditorium was equipped with another new invention, air conditioning.

Westinghouse provided the seven foot tall "Electro the Moto-Man". This was a robot that could talk and perform other tasks. Meanwhile, in the Communications Zone, AT&T was showing off a mechanized, synthetic voice that could speak to fairgoers. IBM had new devices of their own, such as the electric typewriter and an electric calculator.

Aside from the many exhibits, there were also live shows featuring dancers and other forms of entertainment. The Amusement Zone provided a variety of rides similar to the ones found at fairs in today's world. One of the most popular rides was the parachute jump, which allowed people to experience the exhilaration of dropping from a parachute.

The World of Tomorrow

Each day, the mayor of New York City, Fiorello La Guardia, would roam the grounds and greet fairgoers or entertain celebrity visitors. Franklin Roosevelt visited the fair on its opening day and even officially "opened" the event. King George VI and Queen Elizabeth of England also visited the fair.

The New York World's Fair was hugely popular. On its first day, nearly 200,000 people paid to enter the gates. By the end of the fair's existence in 1940, more than 44 million people had visited the "World of Tomorrow".

This streamlined locomotive was one of many exhibits on display during the World's Fair. It ran at 60 mph (stationary) throughout the duration of the fair.

About the Author:

Jake Henderson is a graduate of Southwestern Oklahoma State University in Weatherford, OK, where he earned a BA in History Education. He also has a Master's Degree in History Education from SWOSU, which he earned in 2004. He has taught US History, World History, AP Government, US Government, Geography, Oklahoma History, and Psychology at the High School level for more than fifteen years. He currently lives and teaches in Woodward, OK.

Printed in Great Britain
by Amazon